CHICAGO
BEARS

by George Castle

Published by ABDO Publishing Company, 8000 West 78th Street, Edina, Minnesota 55439. Copyright © 2011 by Abdo Consulting Group, Inc. International copyrights reserved in all countries. No part of this book may be reproduced in any form without written permission from the publisher. SportsZone™ is a trademark and logo of ABDO Publishing Company.

Printed in the United States of America,
North Mankato, Minnesota
062010
092010

Editor: Matt Tustison
Copy Editor: Nicholas Cafarelli
Interior Design and Production: Christa Schneider
Cover Design: Kazuko Collins

Photo Credits: David Stluka/AP Images, cover; John Swart/AP Images, title page; Red McLendon/AP Images, 4; Fred Jewell/AP Images, 6; Mike Roemer/ AP Images, 9; Phil Sandlin/AP Images, 11, 43 (middle); AP Images, 12, 15, 17, 18, 21, 23, 25, 26, 31, 42 (top, middle, and bottom), 43 (top), 44; NFL Photos/ AP Images, 29, 33; Amy Sancetta/AP Images, 34, 43 (bottom); Andy Manis/AP Images, 36; Paul Spinelli/AP Images, 39, 47; Kevork Djansezian/AP Images, 41

Library of Congress Cataloging-in-Publication Data
Castle, George.
  Chicago Bears / George Castle.
      p. cm. — (Inside the NFL)
  ISBN 978-1-61714-006-8
  1. Chicago Bears (Football team)—History—Juvenile literature. I. Title.
  GV956.C5C37 2010
  796.332'640977311—dc22
                          2010016175

TABLE OF CONTENTS

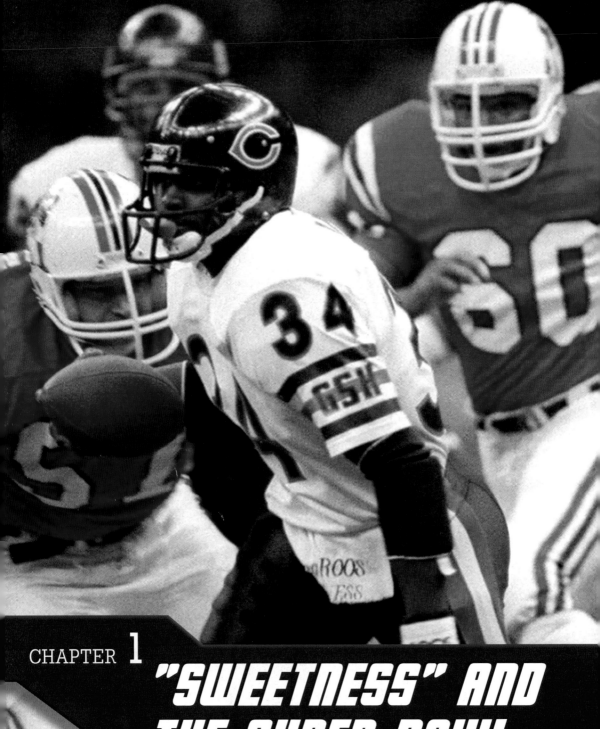

CHAPTER 1

"SWEETNESS" AND THE SUPER BOWL

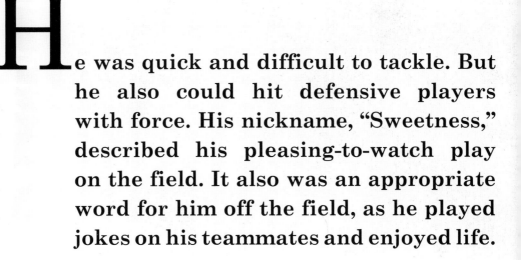

He was quick and difficult to tackle. But he also could hit defensive players with force. His nickname, "Sweetness," described his pleasing-to-watch play on the field. It also was an appropriate word for him off the field, as he played jokes on his teammates and enjoyed life.

He was Walter Payton, perhaps the greatest player in Bears history.

Payton was not well known at the beginning of his National Football League (NFL) career. He had played at Jackson State, a historically African-American college in Mississippi. Jackson State did not compete against the largest schools in the country. But the game films could not lie. Payton was a sure thing. So in the 1975 NFL Draft, new Bears general manager Jim Finks selected him in the first round, fourth overall. Payton was the first key player in a long process that built the Bears into Super Bowl champions.

WALTER PAYTON RUNS WITH THE BALL DURING CHICAGO'S 46–10 ROUT OF NEW ENGLAND IN SUPER BOWL XX. AFTER A DECADE OF NFL STARDOM, PAYTON WAS FINALLY PART OF A CHAMPIONSHIP TEAM.

WALTER PAYTON GAINS SOME OF HIS 275 RUSHING YARDS IN THE BEARS'
10–7 WIN OVER THE VIKINGS IN NOVEMBER 1977.

Payton had an average rookie season. But he emerged as a top NFL running back in 1976 with 1,390 rushing yards. In 1977, Payton led the Bears to their first playoff appearance since 1963. He gained 1,852 yards and averaged 5.5 yards per carry. Included was a November 20 game at Soldier Field in which Payton ran for 275 yards, then an NFL record. This helped the Bears edge the Minnesota Vikings 10–7.

"You Chicago people are spoiled by Payton—he's a phenomenon," longtime Vikings coach Bud Grant said.

Payton gained thousands of rushing yards while the Bears' performance was average, or worse. Chicago made the playoffs with a 9–5 record in 1977. But the Bears slumped in 1978. They went back to the postseason with a 10–6 mark in 1979. They then had four mediocre years in a row. But the team steadily gathered talent, largely through the draft.

Defensive end Dan Hampton arrived in 1979. Linebacker Mike Singletary came aboard in 1981. Quarterback Jim McMahon was taken in 1982. Defensive end Richard Dent, defensive back Dave Duerson, tackle Jimbo Covert, and wide receiver Willie Gault were part of a strong draft class in

MORE ON "SWEETNESS"

In addition to his rushing and receiving skills, Walter Payton was a surprisingly good passer on trick plays. He completed 11 of 34 attempts in his career and threw eight touchdown passes, including one to quarterback Jim McMahon in a game in 1985.

Payton was also famous for repeatedly running up a steep hill in Arlington Heights, Illinois, in the off-season to improve his conditioning. When asked in 1983 about the secret of his success, Payton replied, "Not staying in one place for very long."

After he retired, Payton served as a volunteer assistant basketball coach at a high school in Schaumburg, Illinois, among other activities. His son, Jarrett Payton, played running back briefly in the NFL for the Tennessee Titans in 2005.

1983. That draft was Finks's last as Chicago's general manager. Seven players who would start on the 1985 Super Bowl XX team came from the 1983 draft.

The most important non-player move was owner George Halas's hiring of Mike Ditka as coach in early 1982. Halas was impressed by a letter Ditka wrote in which he expressed a desire to coach the team for which he had

WHY THE "46" DEFENSE?

The Bears' remarkable defense in the 1985 season was called the "46" defense. It was named after the No. 46 uniform number of tough safety Doug Plank, who actually had not played for the team since 1982. Buddy Ryan became Chicago's defensive coordinator in 1978. He created the 46 defense in 1981. The defense featured a unique front, designed to confuse the quarterback. The defensive line was shifted dramatically to the weak side—the opposite end from the offense's tight end. This front made it considerably harder for offensive lines to execute blocking assignments.

played in the 1960s. By 1984, the Bears had put together a winning squad. But it was too late for Halas to enjoy. "Papa Bear" died at 88 on October 31, 1983.

The defense, built by defensive coordinator Buddy Ryan, allowed just 248 points in 16 games in 1984. That year, the Bears won their first division title since 1963. They played even better in 1985. They gave up only 198 points in 16 games. The Bears became a national sensation by starting out 12–0. Included in this stretch were back-to-back shutouts of the Dallas Cowboys and the Atlanta Falcons by a combined 80–0.

Everyone paid attention to 300-pound William "Refrigerator" Perry, the team's top draft choice in 1985. Despite his size, "The Fridge" was athletic enough to dunk a basketball. Ditka decided to settle some old

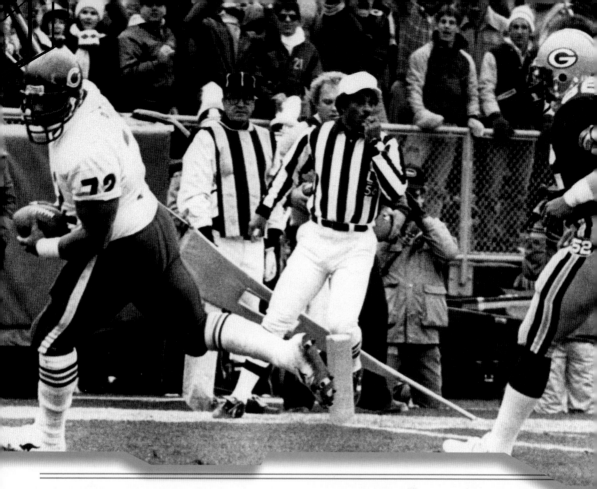

THE BEARS' WILLIAM PERRY GOES INTO THE END ZONE FOR A TOUCHDOWN AHEAD OF THE PACKERS' GEORGE CUMBY ON NOVEMBER 3, 1985.

grudges from his playing days with Green Bay Packers coach Forrest Gregg. He used Perry, a defensive tackle, at fullback to score a rushing touchdown in the Bears' 23–7 home win over the Packers in a *Monday Night Football* game on October 21. Two weeks later, Ditka had Perry line

NICKNAMES

A lot of nicknames besides "Sweetness" and "The Fridge" were given to the 1985 Bears players, especially on defense: "Danimal" for defensive end Dan Hampton, "Mongo" for defensive tackle Steve McMichael, "Samurai Mike" for linebacker Mike Singletary, "LA Mike" for cornerback Mike Richardson, "Double-D" for safety Dave Duerson, and, last but not least, "Punky QB" for Jim McMahon.

up on offense again, this time in Green Bay. He caught a 4-yard touchdown pass from McMahon.

Star quarterback Dan Marino and the Miami Dolphins spoiled Chicago's bid for a perfect 1985 season with a 38–24 victory on *Monday Night Football*. The loss did not stop some of the Bears, led by Payton and Singletary, from taping the famed "Super Bowl Shuffle" video rap session the next day. Such was the confidence of this team.

The Bears won their final three regular-season games to finish a team-best 15–1. But the best was yet to come. In the postseason, the defense shut out the New York Giants and the Los Angeles Rams at Soldier Field. Chicago won those games by a combined 45–0. Now it was on to the Super Bowl in New Orleans, Louisiana. It seemed that the whole world was watching the colorful Bears. They did not disappoint. They routed the New England Patriots 46–10 in front of 73,818 on January 26, 1986, in the Superdome. The Bears scored in the air and on the ground, including on a 1-yard run by Perry. The only disappointment for Bears fans was that Ditka did not call a play on which Payton could score.

It was a season that could hardly be repeated—and it was not. The defense was actually even stingier in allowing just 187 points in a 14–2 season in 1986. But the Bears had quarterback problems. McMahon battled

FROM LEFT, WILLIE GAULT, STEVE MCMICHAEL, COACH MIKE DITKA, WILLIAM PERRY, AND MAURY BUFORD ARE SUPER BOWL XX CHAMPIONS.

injuries. From the 1986 season through 1991, the Bears won just two of seven playoff games in which they participated. They would never return to the Super Bowl under Ditka. He was fired after a 5–11 season in 1992. But Chicago would never forget 1985.

One by one, the 1985 Bears retired or moved on to other teams. No one was missed more, of course, than Payton. He retired after his thirteenth season in 1987 with an NFL-record 16,726 rushing yards. His 125 total touchdowns were the second most in league history at that point.

Payton might have been the most beloved player in the history of a franchise that went back to the beginning of the NFL.

CHAPTER 2

NEW TEAM, NEW LEAGUE

One of the United States' most popular pro sports teams, the Bears, and the most popular sports league, the NFL, began in an unlikely way. Both were founded by a man who had played right field for the New York Yankees before Babe Ruth.

All of this happened in 1920. George Halas was a native of Chicago's West Side and a University of Illinois graduate. He had spent two months of the 1919 season as a Yankees outfielder. He played a few games in right field and hit just .091. Ruth arrived the next season. The rest was history—in baseball. Obviously not cut out for baseball, Halas looked for work.

Industrialist A. E. Staley was eager to field a competitive football team for his cornstarch company in Decatur, Illinois. He contacted Halas after getting a recommendation from University of Illinois football star Ed "Dutch" Sternaman. Halas worked as a Staley employee and a player-coach of the new team. Halas and Sternaman recruited top college talent from all over

GEORGE HALAS, SHOWN IN 1933, WAS A KEY FIGURE IN THE CREATION OF THE BEARS FRANCHISE AND THE NFL IN 1920. HE REMAINED INVOLVED WITH THE TEAM UNTIL HIS DEATH IN 1983.

the Midwest. At the same time, Canton (Ohio) Bulldogs owner Ralph Hay wanted to organize a professional football league. Halas figured his new team, the Decatur Staleys, ought to join. The organizers met at Hay's Hupmobile car dealership in Canton on September 17, 1920.

The men formed the American Professional Football Association (APFA). Joining the Staleys were the Bulldogs, Akron Pros, Buffalo All-Americans, Chicago Cardinals, Chicago Tigers, Cleveland Tigers, Columbus Panhandles, Dayton Triangles, Detroit Heralds, Hammond Pros, Muncie Flyers, Rochester Jeffersons, and Rock Island Independents. Jim Thorpe was named league president.

The Decatur Staleys finished their first season, in 1920, with a 5–1–2 record in league play and a 10–1–2 mark overall.

YOU DROPPED SOMETHING

George Halas set an NFL record in 1923 that stood until 1972: longest return of a fumble for a touchdown at 98 yards. Who was the fumbler? It was the legendary Jim Thorpe, then playing for the Oorang Indians. Thorpe had been an Olympic champion in the pentathlon and decathlon. He had also played professional baseball and basketball.

The Staleys tied Akron 0–0 in a playoff game at Wrigley Field in Chicago.

The Staleys moved to Chicago full time in 1921 when Staley decided to not support the team any longer. However, he gave Halas and Sternaman $5,000 in "seed money" to move the team to the big city. The two owners struck a deal for the use of Wrigley Field for 15 percent of ticket profits. Then, in 1922, Halas and Sternaman dropped the name Staleys in favor of the Bears. The Chicago Cubs baseball team was already playing

SHOWN IN 1930, RED GRANGE, *LEFT*, AND BRONKO NAGURSKI FORMED A STRONG COMBINATION IN THE BEARS' BACKFIELD.

at Wrigley Field. Halas figured football players are bigger than baseball players. Since bears are larger versions of cubs, Halas decided to call his football team the Bears. In 1922, the APFA also chose a new name: the National Football League (NFL).

The Bears and the NFL struggled for attention and fans until November 22, 1925. On that date, Halas and Sternaman signed Red Grange. Grange was a University of Illinois player considered the greatest in college football. "The Galloping Ghost" and the Bears were booked on a barnstorming tour with eight games in 12 days. Huge crowds, including 70,000 at New York's Polo Grounds, turned out all over the country. Grange and agent C. C. Pyle split $250,000. The Bears earned $100,000. Both were huge amounts at the time. Soon, bruising fullback Bronko Nagurski joined Grange in the backfield. Halas continued

RED GRANGE

Red Grange met the other biggest name in sports, New York Yankees star Babe Ruth, on his barnstorming tour with the Bears in 1925. "Don't believe anything they write about you, good or bad," Ruth told Grange. "And further, get the dough while the getting is good, but don't break your heart trying to get it. And don't pick up too many checks!" Grange was the most elusive runner in his time in college at the University of Illinois. He actually made more of an impact as a defensive back for the Bears. He played for the team in 1925 and from 1929 through 1934. Grange later provided commentary on TV broadcasts of Bears road games in the early 1960s.

to play for the Bears in addition to coaching them. He played end on offense and defense.

The money from the Grange tour did not last long. The Bears lost $18,000 in the Great Depression year of 1932. That year, they played the first pro football playoff game indoors—at the old Chicago Stadium.

Halas had stopped playing after the 1928 season. But he was still the team's coach and part owner. He wanted to buy out Sternaman to be the Bears' only owner. He barely made a deadline on August 9, 1933, to give Sternaman $38,000. The Bears went on to win the first official NFL title that year with a 23–21 victory over the visiting New York Giants. Chicago lost the NFL Championship Game in 1934 (to the host Giants) and again in 1937 (to the visiting Washington Redskins).

THE GIANTS' DALE BURNETT CLOSES IN ON BEARS BALL CARRIER
BEATTIE FEATHERS IN OCTOBER 1937 AT THE POLO GROUNDS IN NEW YORK.

The best was yet to come. The Bears drafted a quarterback named Sid Luckman out of Columbia University in 1939. Luckman's arrival led to the longest winning era in team history.

STAYING INDOORS

Arena football was still 54 years away when the Bears and Portsmouth Spartans played the first indoor title game in 1932. But the improvised field in Chicago Stadium was like arena ball: only 80 yards long. Hash marks were first used in this game and straw was put over the surface, which had just hosted a circus. The Bears won 9–0.

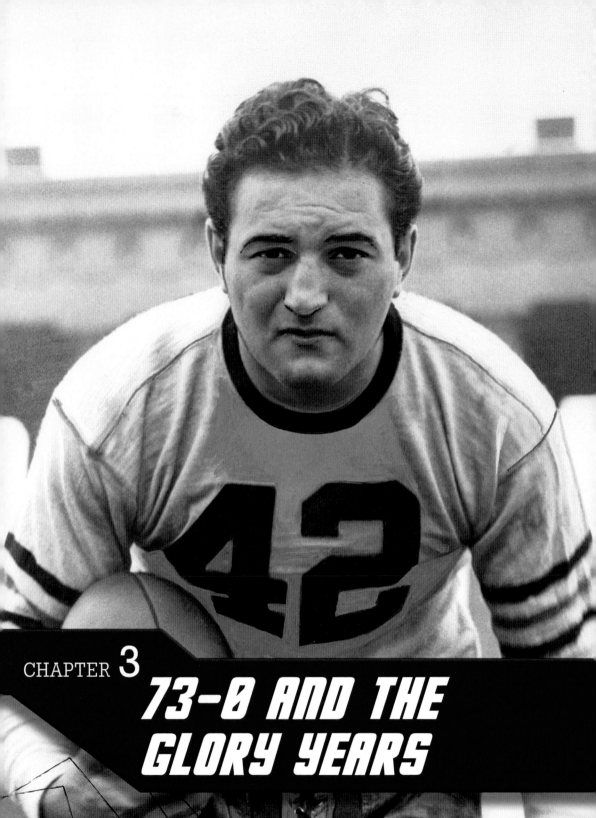

CHAPTER 3

73-0 AND THE GLORY YEARS

W hen George Halas signed Sid Luckman in 1939, he knew he had the man to help him change pro football.

The NFL game was centered on running the ball in a "single-wing" formation. Most teams did not pass much. But Halas devised a "T-formation." In this formation, a quarterback lined up with two running backs behind him and had the option of passing or running. The smart Luckman was just the man to head up the "T-formation." It later was celebrated in the team fight song "Bear Down, Chicago Bears."

"There was all the spinning for handoffs or fakes, and new signal-calling," Luckman remembered of learning the complicated new system. "All the fundamentals were different from what I had played as a tailback."

BEARS QUARTERBACK SID LUCKMAN, SHOWN DURING HIS ROOKIE SEASON IN OCTOBER 1939, HELPED MAKE PASSING THE BALL MORE POPULAR IN THE NFL.

Luckman played part time in 1939. He then became the starter in 1940. The Bears excelled as a result. Backs Bill Osmanski, George McAfee, and Ray Nolting and linemen Bulldog Turner, Joe Stydahar, Danny Fortmann, and George Musso helped Luckman. Chicago headed for a showdown with the equally powerful Washington Redskins and quarterback "Slingin'" Sammy Baugh in the championship game. After an earlier 7–3 Redskins win, owner George Preston Marshall said the Bears were "quitters . . . just a bunch of crybabies. They fold up when the going gets tough."

Inspired by the insult, the Bears took out their frustrations on the Redskins with Marshall watching helplessly at old Griffith Stadium in Washington. Osmanski ran 68 yards for a touchdown early. The Bears

HUMOR IN SAD TIMES

In the Redskins' famous 73–0 loss to the Bears in the 1940 NFL Championship Game, Washington missed a chance to score when Charley Malone could not catch a pass from Sammy Baugh in the first quarter. Chicago was ahead just 7–0 at the time. Baugh was asked afterward whether the outcome would have been different had Malone hung on to the ball. "Yes, the score would have been 73–6," Baugh quipped.

scored so often, Luckman's strong right arm was hardly needed. The Bears ran all over the 'Skins in the most lopsided championship game ever—a 73–0 massacre. Chicago defenders ran back three interceptions for touchdowns.

The legendary victory established the Bears as "The Monsters of the Midway." They were on course to win three more championships in the next five years with Luckman at the controls. The team was even more dominating in 1941 with a 10–1

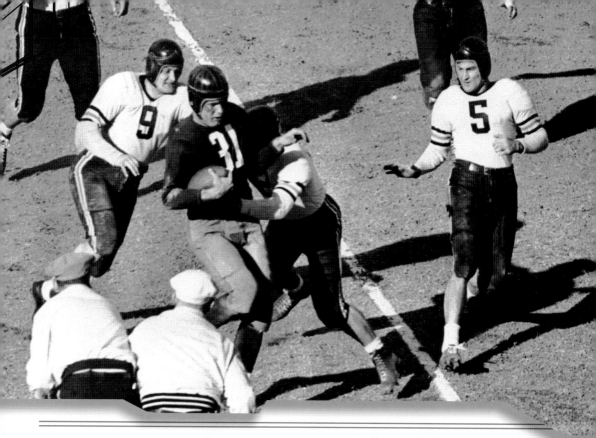

SID LUCKMAN, WHO ALSO PLAYED DEFENSE, TACKLES THE REDSKINS' JOHNNY JOHNSTON IN THE BEARS' 73–0 ROUT IN THE 1940 NFL TITLE GAME.

regular season. Chicago tied the archrival Green Bay Packers for the Western Division title. The Bears dominated the Packers 33–14 in a divisional playoff game before more than 43,000 at Wrigley Field. A week later, just 13,341 showed up to watch the Bears thump the Giants 37–9 in the NFL title game.

FIGHT SONG

The famed fight song "Bear Down, Chicago Bears," written by Al Hoffman, made its debut in 1941. It remains one of the most stirring team songs in any sport. "Bear Down, Chicago Bears" is part of a list of memorable Chicago team songs that include "Go, Cubs, Go" for the North Side baseball team, "Let's Go-Go-Go, White Sox" for the South Side baseball squad, and "Here Come the Hawks" for the National Hockey League team.

SID LUCKMAN

A month and a half before his five-touchdown-pass performance in the 1943 NFL Championship Game, Sid Luckman had played even better.

In a contest on November 14, 1943, on "Sid Luckman Day" honoring the native New Yorker at the Polo Grounds, Luckman threw a record seven touchdown passes against the Giants. Luckman did this despite a sore shoulder that he had injured the week before.

Luckman played in the NFL until 1950, when the Bears tried to replace him with former University of Notre Dame standout Johnny Lujack. Lujack only lasted one more season with the team.

Loyal to George Halas, Luckman later joined the Bears as an assistant coach. He helped the linebackers as well as the quarterbacks. He also started in the business world in Chicago. He died at age 81 on July 5, 1998.

Halas had left for U.S. Navy service for the 1943 season. But Luckman stayed on to lead the Bears to an 8–1–1 record. The title-clinching game had been spurred by Bronko Nagurski. Nagurski had come out of a six-year retirement to play tackle. He helped fill in for players away in the military. Switching to his old fullback position, "The Bronk" rushed for 84 fourth-quarter yards on 16 carries. The Bears rallied for a 35–24 win over the cross-town Chicago Cardinals in the regular-season finale. Then Luckman put on a show against Baugh and the Redskins in the title game at Wrigley Field. Luckman threw five touchdown passes in a 41–21 triumph.

BRONKO NAGURSKI WORKS OUT AT WRIGLEY FIELD IN 1943. NAGURSKI CAME OUT OF RETIREMENT THAT YEAR AND HELPED THE BEARS WIN THE NFL TITLE.

The Bears slipped a bit in 1944 and 1945. By this time, Luckman was serving in the U.S. Navy but still stationed in the United States. He could not practice with the team during the week. But he could play in Chicago's games on the weekends. By 1946, he was able to return to the team full time. That year, the Bears returned as strong as ever. They finished 8–2–1. Halas was back as coach as well. This time they faced the Giants for the title. Going back to his old tailback days, Luckman was able to use his legs for the title. He employed a rarely used trick play called "Bingo-Keep-It."

"When I got the snap, I faked to [George] McAfee and he headed around left end with the Giants in wild pursuit," Luckman said. "I just tucked the ball against my leg and danced around right end. I got two great blocks from [Bulldog] Turner and [Ray] Bray and went the 19 yards for a touchdown." The visiting Bears won 24–14.

The Bears continued to contend for the Western Division title before the end of Luckman's career in 1950. But they did not get back to an NFL title game. Their greatest era had ended. But the Bears' place among pro football legends was secure.

HALL OF FAMERS

George Halas, Sid Luckman, George McAfee, George Musso, Bronko Nagurski, Joe Stydahar, and Bulldog Turner—who all coached or played for Bears championship teams in the 1940s—went on to make the Pro Football Hall of Fame. The numbers of Halas, Luckman, McAfee, Nagurski, and Turner have been retired by the Bears.

COACH GEORGE HALAS AND QUARTERBACK SID LUCKMAN ARE SHOWN THE DAY BEFORE THE BEARS' 24–14 WIN OVER THE GIANTS IN THE 1946 NFL TITLE GAME.

CHAPTER 4

A TOUGH TEAM

In the seasons after Sid Luckman retired, the Bears were not known for quarterbacks. Rather, they established an identity as a bruising squad that would leave you battered no matter the final score. Sometimes, that was the Bears' biggest accomplishment. They had three losing seasons in the 1950s.

George Halas made mistakes in judging quarterbacks. He drafted and then traded Bobby Layne. Layne became a star on championship Detroit Lions teams. Halas kept former Notre Dame star Johnny Lujack instead of Layne. George Blanda was a Bears backup through much of the 1950s. He was released and then became a star with the Houston Oilers in the new American Football League in 1960. Ed Brown, an average player, became the Bears' starting quarterback throughout the second half of the 1950s. He threw to skilled ends Harlon Hill and Jim Dooley.

The best-known, and perhaps toughest, Bear of the decade

LINEBACKER BILL GEORGE, SHOWN IN 1963, WAS A BEARS STANDOUT FROM 1952 TO 1965. HE AND THE TEAM EARNED A HARD-NOSED REPUTATION.

was middle guard Bill George. He started playing for the team in 1952. George invented the position of middle linebacker by playing off the line. He backed up end Ed Sprinkle, dubbed "The Meanest Man in Football" by *Colliers* magazine.

"A lot said I played dirty," Sprinkle said. "That's just not true. Mean maybe, but not dirty. . . . A guy wouldn't have lasted very long in the league if he played dirty regularly."

George was the defense's star. Fullback Rick Casares provided toughness on offense. The Bears finally reached another NFL title game. But they were wiped out 47–7 by the host New York Giants on December 30, 1956. Halas had turned over the head coach's job for two years to Paddy Driscoll. The Bears finished 8–4 in four other seasons in the 1950s. But they always fell short of the playoffs.

The Bears fell further back when the Green Bay Packers became powerful NFL champions under coach Vince Lombardi in the early 1960s. A 49–0 Packers thrashing of the Bears in 1962 greatly upset Halas.

Halas aggressively prepared his defense in 1963 to stop Green Bay stars Bart Starr, a quarterback, and Jim Taylor, a fullback. The defense was led by George and fellow linebackers Joe Fortunato and Larry Morris, linemen Doug Atkins and Stan Jones, and defensive backs Rosey Taylor and Dave Whitsell.

RONNIE BULL TAKES OFF ON A RUN AGAINST THE GIANTS DURING THE BEARS' 14–10 WIN IN THE 1963 NFL TITLE GAME AT WRIGLEY FIELD.

All rose to the occasion like never before. The defense allowed just 144 points in 14 games.

Meanwhile, tight end Mike Ditka and wide receiver Johnny Morris chipped in with clutch catches. The Bears won the Western Division with an 11–1–2 record. They again met the Giants in the title game. This time the contest was at a frozen Wrigley Field on December 29, 1963. The temperature was just nine degrees. Again, the defense held firm in a 14–10 victory. The Bears battered veteran Giants quarterback Y. A. Tittle. Thousands of fans who could not get into Wrigley Field watched on closed-circuit TV at theaters around the Chicago area. The game telecast was blacked out on local over-the-air TV.

The title would be Halas's last as Bears coach. Chicago was hurt by injuries and the tragic deaths of running back Willie Galimore and wide receiver John "Bo" Farrington in an offseason automobile accident. The Bears went just 5–9 in 1964.

They had a brief revival when they came away with the best draft class in team history. Linebacker Dick Butkus was a Chicago native out of the University of Illinois. Running back Gale Sayers played at the University of Kansas. Butkus, taken third overall in the first round, was an immediate star on defense in 1965. Sayers, selected

fourth overall in the first round, stunned the NFL with a record 22 touchdowns as a rookie. His greatest game was on December 12, 1965. That day, via runs and punt and kickoff returns, he scored six touchdowns in a 61–20 win over the San Francisco 49ers at Wrigley Field. He could have scored a seventh touchdown. But Halas kept him out of the game late for fear of injury.

Sayers was such an elusive runner that defenders thought they had stopped him before finding out he had slipped away.

MADE INTO A MOVIE

The friendship between Gale Sayers and fellow Bears running back Brian Piccolo, who died of cancer at age 26 in 1970, was made into the famed 1971 ABC-TV movie Brian's Song. Billy Dee Williams and James Caan starred. Jack Warden played George Halas.

THE BEARS WERE MEDIOCRE IN THE LATE 1960s. BUT RUNNING BACK GALE SAYERS PROVIDED PLENTY OF THRILLS FOR THE TEAM'S FANS.

DICK BUTKUS

Dick Butkus was the most authentic Chicago Bear. He grew up on the far southeast side of the city and attended Chicago Vocational High School. He played fullback in addition to linebacker in high school. Staying close to home, Butkus then starred for the University of Illinois.

Those good hands on offense led him to play on special teams in the NFL. Butkus actually caught two point-after-touchdown passes when the attempted kicks failed.

He turned his terror-on-the-field reputation into money after his pro football career. Nicknamed "Super Crunch" for his violent style at middle linebacker, Butkus moved to Hollywood and became an actor after his last Bears game in 1973.

Butkus and Gale Sayers were both drafted by the Bears in 1965, one pick apart. Their numbers (Butkus's 51 and Sayers's 40) were retired together during a game in 1994.

"It was on an 80-yard run on a screen pass he made against us," Los Angeles Rams tackle Rosey Grier said. "I hit him so hard near the line of scrimmage, I thought my shoulder must have busted him in two. I heard a roar from the crowd, and when I looked up he was 15 yards down the field and going for the score."

Despite having Sayers and Butkus, the Bears were average. Halas finally retired as coach in early 1968. He turned over the team to longtime assistant coach Jim Dooley. But Chicago collapsed in 1969. The Bears finished 1–13, the worst record in team history.

Between 1969 and 1975, Chicago had a 28–69–1 record. Sayers's and Butkus's Hall of Fame careers ended early because of knee injuries. Mediocre quarterback play prevailed.

DICK BUTKUS, SHOWN IN 1971, WAS A STAR LINEBACKER FOR HIS HOMETOWN BEARS FROM 1965 TO 1973. HE MADE EIGHT PRO BOWLS.

The only real change in the team was leaving Wrigley Field after 50 seasons for the rundown Soldier Field stadium near Lake Michigan in 1971.

Finally, the Halas family had enough of losing. As the 1974 season started, George Halas Jr., then the team president, hired dynamic former Minnesota Vikings general manager Jim Finks to become the Bears' general manager. Finks's first No. 1 draft pick, Walter Payton in 1975, would start the team's long march toward the Super Bowl.

CHAPTER 5

GETTING BACK TO THE SUPER BOWL

The Bears' drafting of star running back Walter Payton in 1975 started a process that ended with the celebrated 1985 team demolishing the New England Patriots in Super Bowl XX. But getting to the Super Bowl, let alone winning one, is never easy.

Chicago won 11 regular-season games or more in five of the six years after the Super Bowl season. But the Bears could not get back to the big game. They would have to start rebuilding after Mike Ditka was fired as coach early in 1993. The team hired Dave Wannstedt to succeed Ditka. Wannstedt had been the Super Bowl champion Dallas Cowboys' defensive coordinator.

After a four-year period in which Jim Harbaugh was the No. 1 quarterback, the Bears worked Erik Kramer and Steve Walsh into the role in 1994. They briefly turned around the team's fortunes. The Bears made the playoffs as a wild-card team at 9–7. They then shocked the rival Minnesota Vikings 35–18 on the road in the first round on January 1, 1995. But the Bears were

QUARTERBACK REX GROSSMAN PICKS UP THE BALL AFTER A FUMBLE DURING CHICAGO'S 29–17 LOSS TO INDIANAPOLIS IN SUPER BOWL XLI IN FEBRUARY 2007. IT WAS THE BEARS' FIRST SUPER BOWL APPEARANCE IN 21 YEARS.

QUARTERBACK ERIK KRAMER PREPARES TO PASS DURING THE BEARS' 14–6
WIN OVER THE VIKINGS IN OCTOBER 1995.

knocked out of the postseason the next week in a 44–15 loss to the host San Francisco 49ers.

Chicago started 6–2 but finished with only a 9–7 record in 1995 and missed the playoffs. The team wasted Kramer's 29 touchdown passes against just 10 interceptions. He threw for a team-record 3,838 yards. The Bears had a pair of 1,000-yard receivers: Curtis Conway and Jeff Graham.

Unfortunately for the Bears, Kramer got hurt and the quarterback position became unstable again. Wannstedt was fired in late 1998 after two 4–12 seasons in a row.

Dick Jauron replaced Wannstedt. Jauron could not turn the Bears around until a surprising 2001 season. This entire era of decline was made even worse by the sad news of Payton's death at age 45 from a rare liver disease on November 1, 1999.

The Bears came out of nowhere to stun the NFL in 2001. Quarterback Jim Miller completed 57.7 percent of his passes and threw for 13 touchdowns. Rookie Anthony Thomas was another surprise with 1,183 rushing yards. Chicago finished 13–3 and won the National Football Conference (NFC) Central. But the fairy tale came to an end with a 33–19 home loss to the Philadelphia Eagles in the divisional round of the playoffs.

That was the last game at Soldier Field for a year. The legendary lakefront stadium was reconstructed in 2002. In the meantime, the Bears played their home games at the University of Illinois in Champaign. Chicago was 4–12, 7–9, and 5–11 in the next three seasons. Before the 2004 season, they again changed coaches. They replaced Jauron with Lovie Smith. Smith had been the St. Louis Rams' defensive

MUSICAL CHAIRS AT QB

Three different quarterbacks had at least 174 pass attempts for the Bears in 1999. Shane Matthews was busiest (275), followed by rookie Cade McNown (235) and then Jim Miller (174). Matthews threw 10 touchdown passes, McNown eight, and Miller seven. Then, in 2004, four different quarterbacks—Chad Hutchinson, Craig Krenzel, Jonathan Quinn, and Rex Grossman—threw at least 84 passes. The Bears have gone through many dozens of names through the decades in attempting to replace Sid Luckman with another quarterback of his stature.

coordinator. Slowly but surely, the Bears started building a quality defense. It was led by middle linebacker Brian Urlacher. He was the team's top draft pick (first round, ninth overall) in 2000. Lance Briggs joined Urlacher at linebacker. Safety Mike Brown anchored the secondary. Tommie Harris, a tackle, became the leader of the defensive line. The Bears jumped to 11–5 and an NFC North title in 2005. But they lost 29–21 to the visiting Carolina Panthers in the playoffs' divisional round.

The Bears then took the next step, aiming for their return to the Super Bowl in 2006 with a 13–3 season. Chicago was boosted by a great first half of the season from quarterback Rex Grossman. He was a controversial figure who had either been injured or inconsistent since the Bears drafted him in the first round in 2003. Grossman threw for 23 touchdowns but also had 20 interceptions. Thomas Jones enjoyed a strong season with 1,210 rushing yards. The defense, however, saved the day much of the time. The Bears racked up stirring playoff wins at home against the Seattle Seahawks (27–24 in overtime) and the New Orleans Saints (39–14) to reach Super Bowl XLI

LINEBACKER TRADITION KEEPS GROWING

Brian Urlacher was selected as the NFL Defensive Player of the Year in 2005. This continued a Bears middle linebacker tradition. Mike Singletary won the honor in 1985 and 1988. In his career, Urlacher has scored on a 90-yard fumble return and an 85-yard interception return. Fellow linebacker Lance Briggs, though 2009, had returned three interceptions for touchdowns.

BRIAN URLACHER, SHOWN IN 2005, WAS ANOTHER IN A LONG LINE OF STANDOUT LINEBACKERS FOR THE BEARS.

ALONG CAME JONES

Thomas Jones was perhaps one of the most underrated running backs in a Bears history highlighted by Walter Payton and Gale Sayers.

Between 2004 and 2006, Jones gained 3,493 yards and scored 22 touchdowns rushing. In addition, he caught 118 passes. Those numbers were not far off the Payton–Sayers standards.

But Jones was let go in favor of first-round draft pick Cedric Benson, who ended up playing poorly with Chicago. If the Bears thought Jones was starting to decline because of age, they were wrong. Jones continued to star for the New York Jets. At 31, he gained 1,402 yards in 2009.

For his career, Jones had rushed for 9,217 yards through 2009. The Bears released Benson in 2008. But he then went on to jump-start his career with the Cincinnati Bengals.

against the Indianapolis Colts. The game was held at Dolphin Stadium in Miami, Florida, on February 4, 2007.

The sensational Devin Hester put the Bears ahead 7–0 in the first quarter with a 92-yard kickoff return. Chicago took a 14–6 lead soon afterward. But the Peyton Manning-led Colts scored 16 straight points. The Bears were still in the game. They trailed 22–17 in the fourth quarter. But then cornerback Kelvin Hayden intercepted a pass by Grossman and ran it back 56 yards for a clinching touchdown. Grossman threw another interception, fumbled twice, and had a poor overall game even though he completed 20 of 28 passes. The Bears lost 29–17.

Chicago did not get back to the big game after three more mediocre years. Grossman

REX GROSSMAN WALKS BACK TO THE SIDELINE, PAST CHICAGO COACH
LOVIE SMITH, AFTER THROWING AN INTERCEPTION IN SUPER BOWL XLI.

eventually left as a free agent. The Bears made a trade with the Denver Broncos to acquire promising young quarterback Jay Cutler. Chicago gave up quarterback Kyle Orton and three draft picks, including two in the first round, to get Cutler. Cutler did not have a good season in his first year in Chicago. The Bears finished 7–9 in 2009.

The fans are waiting for Cutler to bring back that feeling of Sid Luckman. That is what makes the Bears special. The past links so easily to the present and provides a guide to the future. The Bears, one of pro sports' most legendary teams, once set high standards. They are always trying to reach them again.

TIMELINE

1920	Bears founder George Halas helps form the American Professional Football Association, which later becomes the NFL, at a Canton, Ohio, auto dealership.
1922	After playing as the Staleys their first two seasons, the team is renamed the Bears.
1925	The first of running back sensation Red Grange's barnstorming tour games is played before 36,000 on November 26 at Wrigley Field.
1933	The Bears beat the visiting New York Giants 23–21 on December 17 in the first NFL Championship Game.
1940	Ten Bears score touchdowns as the Monsters of the Midway massacre the host Washington Redskins 73–0 on December 8 in the NFL title game at Griffith Stadium.
1941	Two weeks after the bombing at Pearl Harbor in Hawaii, the Bears beat the Giants 37–9 on December 21 for the NFL title at Wrigley Field.
1943	Sid Luckman throws five touchdown passes as the Bears defeat the Redskins 41–21 on December 26 for the NFL championship at Wrigley Field.
1946	The Bears beat the Giants 24–14 before a then-record NFL title game crowd of 58,346 on December 15 at New York's Polo Grounds.
1963	The Bears intercept five passes by Y. A. Tittle and edge the Giants 14–10 for the NFL crown on December 29 at Wrigley Field.

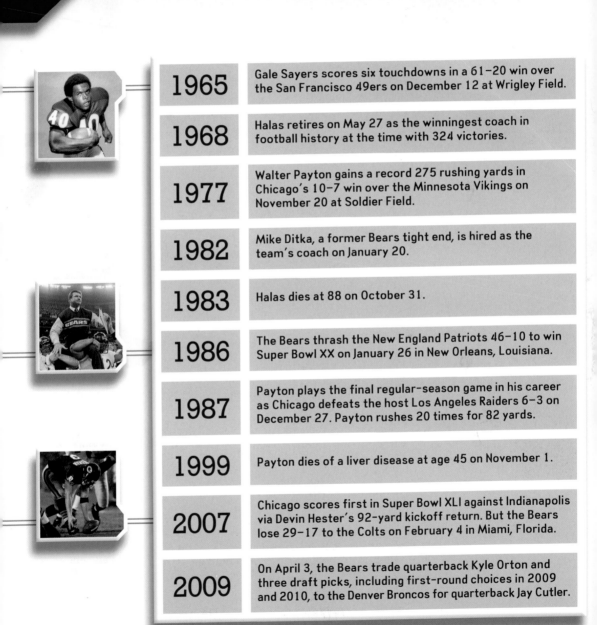

1965	Gale Sayers scores six touchdowns in a 61–20 win over the San Francisco 49ers on December 12 at Wrigley Field.
1968	Halas retires on May 27 as the winningest coach in football history at the time with 324 victories.
1977	Walter Payton gains a record 275 rushing yards in Chicago's 10–7 win over the Minnesota Vikings on November 20 at Soldier Field.
1982	Mike Ditka, a former Bears tight end, is hired as the team's coach on January 20.
1983	Halas dies at 88 on October 31.
1986	The Bears thrash the New England Patriots 46–10 to win Super Bowl XX on January 26 in New Orleans, Louisiana.
1987	Payton plays the final regular-season game in his career as Chicago defeats the host Los Angeles Raiders 6–3 on December 27. Payton rushes 20 times for 82 yards.
1999	Payton dies of a liver disease at age 45 on November 1.
2007	Chicago scores first in Super Bowl XLI against Indianapolis via Devin Hester's 92-yard kickoff return. But the Bears lose 29–17 to the Colts on February 4 in Miami, Florida.
2009	On April 3, the Bears trade quarterback Kyle Orton and three draft picks, including first-round choices in 2009 and 2010, to the Denver Broncos for quarterback Jay Cutler.

QUICK STATS

FRANCHISE HISTORY
Decatur Staleys (1920)
Chicago Staleys (1921)
Chicago Bears (1922–)

SUPER BOWLS
(wins in bold)
1985 (**XX**), 2006 (XLI)

NFL CHAMPIONSHIP GAMES
(wins in bold)
1933, 1934, 1937, **1940**, **1941**, 1942,
1943, **1946**, 1956, **1963**

NFC CHAMPIONSHIP GAMES
(since 1970 AFL-NFL merger)
1984, 1985, 1988, 2006

DIVISION CHAMPIONSHIPS
(since 1970 AFL-NFL merger)
1984, 1985, 1986, 1987, 1988, 1990,
2001, 2005, 2006

KEY PLAYERS
(position, seasons with team)
Doug Atkins (DE, 1955–66)
Dick Butkus (LB, 1965–73)
Danny Fortmann (G, 1936–43)
Bill George (LB, 1952–65)
Red Grange (RB; 1925, 1929–34)
Dan Hampton (DE, 1979–90)
Sid Luckman (QB, 1939–50)
Bronko Nagurski (FB-DT; 1930–37,
    1943)
Walter Payton (RB, 1975–87)
Gale Sayers (RB, 1965–71)
Mike Singletary (LB, 1981–92)
Bulldog Turner (C-LB, 1940–52)
Brian Urlacher (LB, 2000–)

KEY COACHES
Mike Ditka (1982–92):
    106–62–0; 6–6 (playoffs)
George Halas (1920–29, 1933–42,
    1946–55, 1958–67): 318–148–31;
    6–3 (playoffs)

HOME FIELDS
Soldier Field (1971–2001, 2003–)
Memorial Stadium, Champaign,
    Illinois (2002)
Dyche Stadium, Evanston, Illinois
    (1970)
Wrigley Field (1921–70)
Staley Field, Decatur, Illinois (1920)

* All statistics through 2009 season

QUOTES AND ANECDOTES

George Halas had to be careful with his money because he did not have an independent income to support the Bears early on. He almost lost the Bears in 1933 when he barely beat a noon deadline to buy out partner Dutch Sternaman. Halas did it all in the early years, including delivering press releases to Chicago newspapers publicizing his team.

Later, as the Bears were more financially successful, Halas kept his wallet close to him. "George Halas throws nickels around like manhole covers," tight end Mike Ditka said in 1966. Angered, Halas punished Ditka by trading him to the Philadelphia Eagles, one of the NFL's worst teams. But Halas did not hold the grudge for long, as he hired Ditka as the Bears' coach early in 1982.

The Bears' Beattie Feathers became the first NFL player to reach 1,000 rushing yards in a season with 1,004 in 1934. He gained an average of 8.44 yards per carry.

Johnny Morris, one of the Bears' all-time top receivers, later became a prominent TV sportscaster in Chicago. But one of the reasons he went into TV was to add to his modest football income. Morris said his peak Bears salary was $25,000 as a 10-year veteran in the mid-1960s. This was after he had caught an NFL-record 93 passes in 1964. So Morris would practice or play during the day, and then he would go to CBS-owned WBBM-TV to work in the evening.

Walter Payton was known for his versatility. That extended to helping the Bears' office staff. When the regular Halas Hall receptionist went to lunch, Payton sometimes took over and answered the phones. His teammates had to have eyes in the back of their heads because "Sweetness" also was the biggest prankster on the team.

GLOSSARY

archrival

An opponent that brings out great emotion in a team and its players.

berth

A place, spot, or position, such as in the NFL playoffs.

blackout

The prohibition of televising a game in the city in which it is being played if a team does not sell out its home game.

draft

A system used by professional sports leagues to select new players in order to spread incoming talent among all teams.

franchise

An entire sports organization, including the players, coaches, and staff.

free agent

A player free to sign with any team of his choosing after his contract expires.

general manager

The executive who is in charge of the team's overall operation. He or she hires and fires coaches, drafts college players, and signs free agents.

hall of fame

A place built to honor noteworthy achievements by athletes in their respective sports.

mediocre

Neither good nor bad.

postseason

Games played in the playoffs by the top teams after the regular-season schedule has been completed.

rookie

A first-year professional athlete.

rout

An overwhelming defeat.

showdown

A long-anticipated battle between two good or great players or teams.

Further Reading

Chicago Tribune. *The '85 Bears: Still Chicago's Team*. Chicago: Triumph Books, 2005.

Whittingham, Richard. *The Bears: A 75-Year Celebration*. Dallas: Taylor Publishing, 1994.

Whittingham, Richard. *What Bears They Were: Chicago Bears Greats Talk About Their Teams, Their Coaches, and the Times of Their Lives*. Chicago: Triumph Books, 2002.

Web Links

To learn more about the Chicago Bears, visit ABDO Publishing Company online at **www.abdopublishing.com**. Web sites about the Bears are featured on our Book Links page. These links are routinely monitored and updated to provide the most current information available.

Places to Visit

Bears Training Camp

Olivet Nazarene University
One University Avenue
Bourbonnais, IL 60914
1-800-648-1463
The Bears began holding their training camp on Olivet's campus in 2002. Many of the training camp practices are open to the public in late July and early August.

Pro Football Hall of Fame

2121 George Halas Drive Northwest
Canton, OH 44708
330-456-8207
www.profootballhof.com
This hall of fame and museum highlights the greatest players and moments in the history of the National Football League. As of 2010, 29 people affiliated with the Bears were enshrined, including Dick Butkus, Mike Ditka, Red Grange, George Halas, Sid Luckman, Walter Payton, and Gale Sayers.

Soldier Field

425 East McFetridge Drive
Chicago, IL 60605
312-235-7000
www.chicagobears.com/tickets
This is where the Bears play all their home exhibition, regular-season, and playoff games.

INDEX

About the Author

Lifelong Chicagoan George Castle covered the 1985 Super Bowl champion Bears for NBC Sports and other media outlets. Castle has authored 11 baseball books since 1998, hosts the syndicated weekly "Diamond Gems" radio show, and writes for a variety of print and online outlets.